ALCATRAZ, AS IT WAS ORGANIZED IN ITS EARLY YEARS.

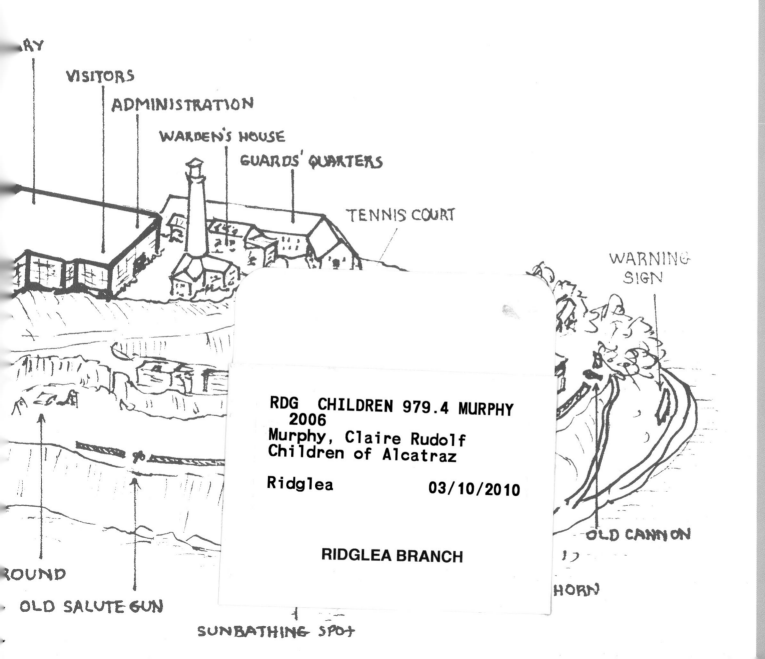

RY

VISITORS

ADMINISTRATION

WARDEN'S HOUSE

GUARDS' QUARTERS

TENNIS COURT

WARNING SIGN

OLD CANNON

ROUND

OLD SALUTE GUN

HORN

SUNBATHING SPOT

Children of
ALCATRAZ

GROWING UP ON THE ROCK

CLAIRE RUDOLF MURPHY

WALKER & COMPANY

New York

For Murph, my rock

This book has only been possible because many former Alcatraz kids have generously shared their memories and photographs. Other stories came from print and film interviews and books written about the island. The ongoing help and support from Chuck Stucker has been invaluable. The early encouragement of Professor Troy Johnson, rangers Lori Brosnan, John Cantwell, and Craig Glassner, and former ranger and military historian John Martini convinced me to persevere. My agent, Liza Voges, believed in this project from the beginning, and my editor, Emily Easton, guided me through to the end. Thanks also to Mary Gruetzke and Kate Sullivan at Walker & Company. My mother-in-law Ann Murphy's place in San Francisco was my home away from home during my research, along with the support of Will and Liam Murphy and Mary Farr. Cousin Anne Lynch helped with library research. My husband, Murph, is my rock and my children, Conor and Megan, my mom and dad, family and friends have patiently listened to my Alcatraz stories for years.

Copyright © 2006 by Claire Rudolf Murphy

First published in the United States of America in 2006 by Walker Publishing Company, Inc.
Distributed to the trade by Holtzbrinck Publishers
For information about permission to reproduce selections from this book,
write to Permissions, Walker & Company, 104 Fifth Avenue, New York, New York 10011

Library of Congress Cataloging-in-Publication Data
Murphy, Claire Rudolf.
Children of Alcatraz : growing up on the rock / Claire Rudolf Murphy.
p.   cm.
Includes bibliographical references and index.
ISBN-10: 0-8027-9577-3 • ISBN-13: 978-0-8027-9577-9 (hardcover)
ISBN-10: 0-8027-9578-1 • ISBN-13: 978-0-8027-9578-6 (reinforced)
1. Alcatraz Island (Calif.)—History—Juvenile literature. 2. Alcatraz Island (Calif.)—Social
life and customs—Juvenile literature. 3. Children—California—Alcatraz Island—History—
Juvenile literature. 4. Children—California—Alcatraz Island—Biography—Juvenile literature.
5. Alcatraz Island (Calif.)—Biography—Juvenile literature. 6. United States Penitentiary,
Alcatraz Island, California—History—Juvenile literature. I. Title.
F868.S156M87 2006   979.4'61—dc22   2006010588
Book design by Alyssa Morris
Visit Walker & Company's Web site at www.walkeryoungreaders.com
Printed in Malaysia
10 9 8 7 6 5 4 3 2 1

All papers used by Walker & Company are natural, recyclable products
made from wood grown in well-managed forests. The manufacturing processes
conform to the environmental regulations of the country of origin.

Warden Swope's Irish setter Pat was the only dog allowed to live on the island during the prison era.

Title page: *This young man eyes the view from the southwest tip of the island from the wooden boardwalk that surrounded Alcatraz, circa 1920.*

CONTENTS

ALCATRAZ KIDS ACKNOWLEDGMENTS:

Lighthouse Era: George Ellenberger, grandson of Vivian Ashford; Wanda Harrington Hart and Jacquie Schneider Campbell

Military Era: Art Butler; Helen Johanson Hansen; Faelyn Lackey, great-granddaughter of Bessie Crabbe; Edy Snyder Lynch; Bill, Ray, and Stan Stewart

Federal Era: Jolene Dollison Babyak, Barbara Chandler Bates, John Brunner, Roy "Rocky" Chandler, Jeanie Comerford, Bill Dolby, Ed Faulk, Kay Bergen Gray-Luttral, Sydney (Sobell) Gureiwitz, Brian Hack, Bud Hart, Ernie Lageson Jr., Barbara Hart Loomis, Don Martin Jr., Bob Orr, Joyce Rose Ritz, Pat Bergen Rothschild, Mark Sobell, Bob Stites, Chuck Stucker, Ruth Faulk Wiley

Indian Occupation: Belva Coltier Belgas; Jon Bellanger; Mike and Peggy Lee Ellenwood; Nan and Angela Lopez; Deynon Means and his mother, LaNada Boyer; Lisa McKay; Asha (Julie) and Adam Nordwall Jr., and their father, Adam Fortunate Eagle Nordwall; Linda Trettevick; and Ed Willie

Thanks also to Ed Burke; Anne Diestel; Federal Bureau of Prisons; Michael Esslinger for his generous help with photographs; photographers Ilka Hartman and Brook Townes; Rose Lawlor Horan of Sacred Heart Cathedral Prepatory; Sharlene Nelson, Joseph Oakes, and Gary Emich of the Alcatraz Challenge; Stacy Peabody, Jon Plutte, Alex, and Sara Sarmiento; Pat Akre, historical photo department, San Francisco Public Library; Gary Fong, photo department *San Francisco Chronicle*; Erica Nordmier and Susan Snyder, historical photo department, University of California, Berkeley; Monique Larre, California Indian Museum and Cultural Center; Lisa Miller and Joe Sanchez, National Archives and Record Administration, Pacific Region.

The many helpful employers of the Golden Gate National Recreational Area include: archaeologist Leo Barker, editor Susan Tasaki, and archivists Susan Ewing Haley and Kim Sulik.

ALCATRAZ PHOTO CREDITS:

Cover: top San Francisco History Center, San Francisco Public Library; bottom left Courtesy Golden Gate National Recreation Area, Park Archives, Kenneth Mickelwait Collection (GOGA-3163); middle Michael Esslinger Collection; right Alcatraz Alumni Association

End papers: Rocky Chandler, from Alcatraz: The Hardest Years 1934-1938.

Front flap, pages 2, 11, bottom 20, middle and bottom 27, 29, 33, 35, 37, bottom 38, bottom left 40, top 41, page 54: Alcatraz Alumni Association

Page 1: Courtesy Golden Gate National Recreation Area, Park Archives, William Elliot Collection (GOGA-40058.007atb)

Pages 4, top 18: Courtesy Golden Gate National Recreation Area, Park Archives, Kenneth Mickelwait Collection (GOGA-3163)

Pages 6, 24, middle 38, 45: National Archives and Records Administration (NARA) Pacific region

Page 7: Brook Landers

Page 8: Courtesy of The Bancroft Library, painting by Louis Choris, University of California, Berkeley

Pages 10, bottom 52, bottom 54: Courtesy Golden Gate National Recreation Area, Park Archives (GOGA-2316)

Page 12: George Ellenberger

Pages 13, 14: Courtesy of The Bancroft Library, Eadweard Muybridge Collection, University of California, Berkeley

Page 15: Faelyn Lackey

Page 16: Mennonite Library and Archives, Bethel College

Page 18, bottom: Wanda Harrington Hart

Page 19, top 20: Edy Snyder Lynch

Page 21, top: Bobby Stewart

Page 21, bottom: Art Butler

Page 23: *San Francisco Chronicle*

Pages 25, 26, top 27: Chandler Collection

Pages 28, 39, top 40, 42: San Francisco History Center, San Francisco Public Library

Pages 30, 34, 36, bottom 43,44, Michael Esslinger Collection

Page 31: Courtesy Golden Gate National Recreation Area, Park Archives, Betty Waller Collection (GOGA 19200)

Page 32: Courtesy Golden Gate National Recreation Area, Park Archives, Carl Sundstrom Collection (GOGA- 3264)

Page 38, top: Ernie Lageson Jr.

Page 40, bottom right: Barbara Hart Catelli

Page 41, bottom: Sacred Heart Cathedral Preparatory

Page 43, top: Jolene Dollison Babyak

Pages 46, top 52: Courtesy Golden Gate National Recreation Area, Park Archives, De Nevi Collection (GOGA-18261); (GOGA-18261)

Page 48: Lori Brosnan

Pages 49, 50, 53, 56: Ilka Hartmann

Pages 51, 54: Brooks Townes

Page 54, bottom: Courtesy Golden Gate National Recreation Area, Park Archives, Office of Resource Management Collection

Pages 57, 59, 60: author

Page 58, top: Emily Easton

Page 58, middle: Liam Murphy

Page 58, bottom: *San Francisco Chronicle*, photographer Fred Larson

INTRODUCTION

A SMALL ISLAND RISES UP in the middle of San Francisco Bay. A mile and a half from the busy city, it stands as a symbol of America's past. Its million-dollar views are among the most spectacular in the world. The winds that sweep through from the Golden Gate and the fog that sometimes blankets the island add to its mystery. Many people think of Alcatraz Island only as the dangerous prison that once housed gangsters like Al Capone and Machine Gun Kelly. Even though the federal prison closed in 1963, people flock to the crumbling cellblock where these notorious criminals once lived, and still live on in Hollywood movies. But nearly two million visitors each year soon discover that Alcatraz is much more than America's Devil's Island. Because of its location near the mouth of the Golden Gate, the first lighthouse and fortification on the West Coast were built here. And in 1969 the empty

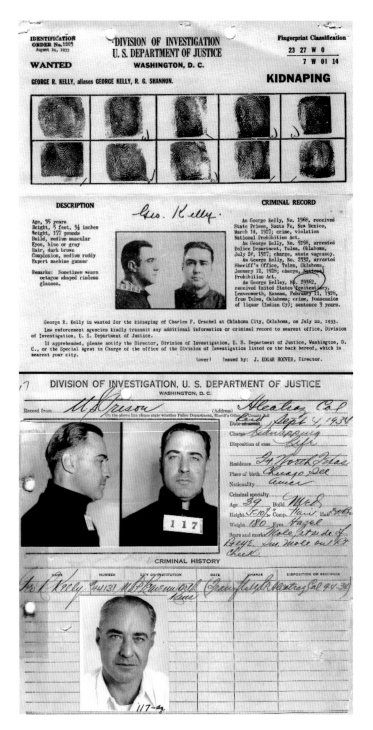

island served as the site of Native American pride and protest during the nineteen-month Indian Occupation.

Residents were rarely interviewed and the truth about life on Alcatraz has often been ignored or shrouded in secrecy. The best kept secret of all is that the children of the lighthouse keepers, army officers, prison guards, and Indian leaders lived here, too.

I first visited Alcatraz in 1974 with my sixth-grade students, a year after it opened to the public. I have returned many times since. A few years ago on a trip with my own children, I discovered that kids had lived on the island. Determined to learn more, I interviewed as many of these former residents as I could find. Almost no information exists about children from the early years of the lighthouse and military eras. Few of the military children are still alive because the army left the island in 1934. Children of the prison guards and lighthouse keepers stay in touch through the Alcatraz Alumni Association, so their stories were more available. Indian children of the Occupation are adults now.

Machine Gun Kelly was one of Alcatraz's most infamous inmates.

Thousands of books have been published about Alcatraz. But the children's stories presented here reveal the island's long history in a new way, as a place not only of prisoners' broken dreams, but also of adventure and community.

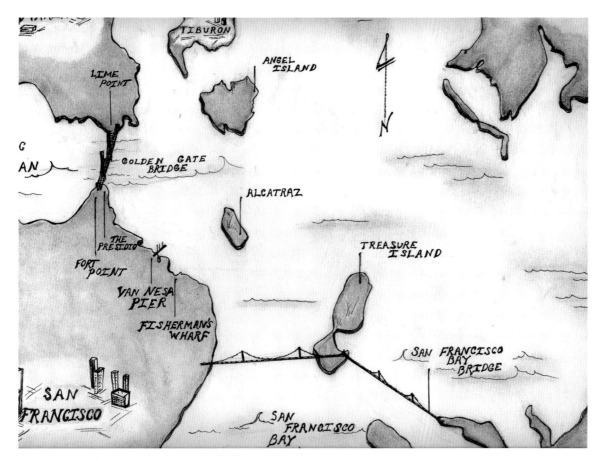

This map shows how close Alcatraz is to San Francisco.

Bateau du port de S.ⁿ Francisco.

Three coastal Miwok are traveling in their tule reed canoe for a day of gathering. The Marin shoreline is in the background.

DIAMOND ISLAND

Before 1854

THOUSANDS OF YEARS AGO Indians of many tribes settled along the shores of San Francisco Bay. The bay teemed with sea life and birds. Ohlone and Miwok people traveled by tule reed canoe to the small island in the middle of the bay. Children fished off its rocky shores and climbed up the high cliffs to collect bird eggs. But most likely no one lived there because it had no fresh water, wild game, or safe harbor.

The Pit River Indians called it *Alisti Ti-Tanin-Mi* or Diamond Island; they believed that a diamond was buried inside the island, which would bring harmony to the world. Some local tribes may have considered the island haunted and banished their wrongdoers to it as punishment.

In 1775 Spanish sailors first sailed into San Francisco Bay and called the island *La Isla de los Alcatraces,* Island of the Pelicans, after the birds that covered the "Rock."

Spanish missionaries arrived soon after and some historians believe Indian families may have hidden on the island to escape being forced to work at their missions. After the Mexican-American War ended in 1848, Alcatraz eventually became the property of the United States government.

This view from San Francisco features Alcatraz in 1853, before the island housed an army post.

A BEACON OF LIGHT

1854 — Present

THE FIRST YOUNG PEOPLE likely to have lived on the island were the children of the lighthouse keepers. Completed in 1854, the new lighthouse guided ships into San Francisco's busy harbor, which was booming since the gold rush five years earlier. Children and grandchildren helped light the lighthouse lamp every evening after filling it with two quarts of sperm whale oil. When electricity came to the island in 1909, kids helped the keepers pull the switches in the lighthouse tower and check the new foghorns around the island. They stood on the cliffs and

Construction of the lighthouse began in December 1852 and was completed on June 1, 1854.

watched the flashing light sweep across the darkened horizon nineteen miles out to sea.

Sixteen-year-old Vivian Ashford arrived in 1913 when her father was transferred from the Point Reyes lighthouse. She enjoyed the monthly dances with boys from San Francisco, and the weekly bowling matches and sewing club meetings. In 1920 she married army officer Lester Hadley in the lighthouse quarters. At her one hundredth birthday party Vivian said, "The happiest days of my life were spent on Alcatraz."

Twenty-three-year-old Vivian Ashford, the daughter of a lighthouse keeper, was married in the lighthouse quarters in 1920.

POST ON ALCATRACES

1859-1907

THE U.S. ARMY began construction of a post on Alcatraces in 1853 to protect the city of San Francisco from invasion by sea. The children of army officers first moved onto the post in 1859. Ten to twenty military offspring roamed the twenty-acre island every year with their friends from the lighthouse. Together they walked along the boardwalk that surrounded the island, roller-skated, played ball, and flew kites on the parade ground where the soldiers also practiced marching. Every morning and evening, families stood at attention

Children helped plant flowers from the mainland in the lovely gardens around the Citadel and the officers' homes.

as soldiers raised and lowered the flag. In the 1880s the children watched as chunks of rocks were blasted from the sides of the island, creating steep cliffs to better protect the fort from invasion.

Ten-year-old Bessie Crabbe moved onto the island in 1888. She loved to draw, play the piano, and walk on top of the seawall with her dear friend, the post surgeon's daughter. Her father, Captain Crabbe, insisted she stop this dangerous activity. Bessie later wrote a school essay about how at first she was angry but later realized her father was trying to protect her. Bessie was heartbroken when her older sister died of scarlet fever. At sixteen she found happiness again when she fell in love with 2nd Lt. George Gatley, enjoying outings with him on and off the island. They married in 1896.

Cannons set up around the island.

The young officer at extreme right is 2nd Lt. George Gatley, with his fiancée, Bessie Crabbe, seated to his right. Behind Bessie is her father, Captain George Crabbe, and to her right is her close friend the post surgeon's daughter.

Inset: Bessie, age fifteen.

These Hopi Indian prisoners were ordered to wear military uniforms while incarcerated.

MILITARY PRISON
1861-1907

ALMOST FROM THE BEGINNING, Alcatraz also housed a military prison, like most army posts. Bessie Crabbe got to know the Hopi Indians imprisoned on Alcatraz in 1894. Their only crime was refusing to let their children be sent to a government boarding school.

Other prisoners were just kids themselves. Fifteen-year-old Walt Stack lied about his age to join the army, but then left his post while stationed in the Philippines in 1925. Locked up on Alcatraz for desertion, he suffered through months of hard labor in the quarry and mistreatment by the older prisoners.

Some of the inmates were dangerous and were kept locked up away from the families. But those convicted of nonviolent crimes like desertion and refusal to serve in the army worked around the island. Some cut the children's hair in the post barbershop. Others, called "pass men," cooked, cleaned, and even babysat for the families. Prisoner Mason accompanied three-year-old Kenneth Mickelwait all over the island, as the young boy checked out the foghorns and watched the ferryboats pass by.

Twice a week the families attended movie screenings right along with the nonviolent convicts in the prisoner's assembly room. Wanda Harrington's grandfather was head lighthouse keeper in the 1920s. Wanda and her friend Jacquie Schneider perched at the prisoners' feet, while the adults sat in wicker chairs along the wall. On her eighth birthday the men showered Wanda with gifts.

Above: Three-year-old Kenneth Mickelwait with prisoner Mason, who is dressed in a baseball suit, in August 1921.

Right: Wanda Harrington with her grandfather, the head lighthouse keeper, waiting for the boat to school in San Francisco.

DISCIPLINARY BARRACKS
1907-34

IN THE EARLY 1900s the army decided Alcatraz was no longer needed to protect San Francisco from invasion by sea. By 1907 a new cell house was completed and most of the armaments were removed from the island. Alcatraz was renamed the Disciplinary Barracks, and operated solely as a military prison until 1934. In the 1920s when Edy Snyder, whose father was a soldier working in the infirmary, was awakened by the long, shrill wail of the escape siren, her mother comforted her by saying, "Don't worry, honey. Some prisoner is tired of being locked up and wants his freedom." One afternoon an escaped prisoner actually hid under Edy's *bed,* but she missed all the excitement because she was at school in San Francisco.

Edy, dressed up in her best clothes, is ready to board the boat for a shopping trip in San Francisco.

Edy was popular with her classmates at Redding School. The students asked her scores of questions about her mysterious island and begged to be invited over. But Edy preferred to explore the island with her best friend, Fay Butler, an officer's daughter. They discovered the perfect spot for hide-and-seek—the island morgue. The other kids never dared to look for the girls there. The caves on the west side of the island were off-limits, but the girls snuck over anyway. One morning Edy's father tried to scare her by reporting that some soldiers had spotted bears in the caves. Later she and Fay found out that another escaped prisoner on the loose tried to hide out there.

Above: *Edy Snyder (right) and her best friend, Fay Butler.*

Left: *The morgue where Edy and Fay played hide-and-seek was never actually used on Alcatraz circa 1910. Dead bodies of soldiers and prisoners were sent over to nearby Angel Island.*

END OF AN ERA *1933-34*

During his five years on the island, teenager Bobby Stewart often delivered messages from the prisoners to their buddies in San Francisco. Had he known, Bobby's father, Major Stewart, the last commanding officer of the Disciplinary Barracks, would have forbidden it. But Bobby saw nothing wrong with his delivery service because the prisoners were his friends. In spring 1933 the prisoners' dance band played at his fourteenth birthday party in the Officers' Club.

Art Butler, Fay's five-year-old brother, liked to help the power plant engineer, Mr. Elliot, operate the big generators. In spring 1933 he also had the perfect place to watch the early construction of the Golden Gate Bridge. In fact, when the bridge was completed in 1937, some of the kids got to roller skate across it before it was opened to cars. Around that same time, the government announced the Disciplinary Barracks would close in August 1934 and a maximum-security penitentiary would

Above right: *Fourteen-year-old Bobby Stewart (in the middle) sits with his buddies Doug and Sheldon Thompson on the dock in 1933.*

Left: *Art Butler enjoyed all the activities on the island.*

open in its place. San Franciscans began protesting the danger of having the worst criminals of the Depression-era crime wave so near the city.

Early one morning Fay's friend Anastasia "Babe" Scott jumped off the Alcatraz dock and swam to San Francisco. Babe's feat alarmed San Franciscans even more. If this girl could swim from Alcatraz, any criminal could, too. But Babe, a champion athlete and swimmer, had waited six months for the right tides and was accompanied by two men in a boat. The campaign against the new prison failed.

By the following summer all the military kids had departed, saying good-bye to the lighthouse kids who remained. Several guard towers were built around the island, more security was added to the cell house, and the army barracks in Building 64 were readied for the new guard families.

MERMAID BESTS TIDES ☆ SETS BAY SWIM PRECEDENT

Girl, 17, Swims From Alcatraz

Crossing Easily Made by Soldier's Daughter

With this long, easy double over-arm crawl, Anastasia Scott conquered the turbulent waters yesterday and successfully swam the distance between Alcatraz Island and the San Francisco mainland, thus establishing herself as the first woman on record to make the crossing. Her time was 43 minutes. At the right Miss Scott is congratulated by Herbert Derham of the Dolphin Club, who acted as her pilot.

Anastasia Scott, 17-year-old San Francisco mermaid, swam from Alcatraz island to the San Francisco mainland yesterday without batting a dusky eyelash

The first woman to swim from the prison island, so far as the records show, and one of the few people who have ever done it, Miss Scott made the crossing of about a mile and a half in 43 minutes, landing safely at the Dolphin Swimming Club dock.

The daughter of Staff Sergeant George A. Scott of the quartermaster corps, stationed at Alcatraz, Miss Scott has won a number of medals for her swimming under the colors of the Western Women's Club.

She said she has wanted to try the swim for some time, but the weather and tides were always against her.

Yesterday morning she told her family she was going fishing, and then, in her own words, she "just jumped off a rock and started swimming at 10 minutes of 10."

She was accompanied by a rowboat containing her pilot, Herbert Derham, and Ralph Davie, both of the Dolphin Club, and Edna Curry, well known local swimmer.

"I had no difficulty at all," she said, "except some of the waves from the ferry boats were pretty big."

Slender, red-haired and full of vivacity, Miss Scott was graduated last year from Galileo High School.

Sunday Blue Laws Scrapped by Atlanta

ATLANTA, Oct. 17 (AP)—Sunday blue laws have been scrapped here.

McPike Will Speak At Democrats' Rally

The Twenty-fifth Assembly District Democratic Club will hold a rally tonight at Taraval Temple.

LINER RUNS AGROUND

MARSEILLES, Oct. 17 (AP)—The British steamer City of Paris went aground tonight 20 miles off the French coast.

PRESENTS CREDENTIALS

ANKARA, Turkey, Oct. 17 (AP)—Robert P. Skinner, new United States Ambassador to Turkey, presented his credentials today

Photo and newspaper article about Anastasia "Babe" Scott's swim from Alcatraz to San Francisco.

DIVISION OF INVESTIGATION, U. S. DEPARTMENT OF JUSTICE
WASHINGTON, D. C.

Record from: *U. S. Penitentiary* (Address) *Alcatraz, Cal*

On the above line please state whether Police Department, Sheriff's Office, or County Jail

Date of arrest *Recd Aug 22, 1934*

Charge *Vio. Income Tax*

Disposition of case *10 yrs*

Residence *Chicago, Ill*

Place of birth *Brooklyn, NY*

Nationality *Ital-American*

Criminal specialty *Hoodlum*

Age *35* Build *Stocky*

Height *5-9* Comp *DK* Hair *Blk slightly bald*

Weight *214* Eyes *Brown*

Scars and marks *Lge ragged cut pear on left side of cheek.*

CRIMINAL HISTORY

NAME	NUMBER	CITY OR INSTITUTION	DATE	CHARGE	DISPOSITION OR SENTENCE
Al house Capone	*40886*	*U.S.P. Atlanta, Ga*	*(Trans to U.S.P. Alcatraz, Cal 8/22/34)*		

Al Capone's prison record.

U.S. PENITENTIARY, ALCATRAZ

1934-63

IN AUGUST 1934 children of the new correctional officers watched the arrival of the first federal prisoners from the balcony of Building 64. Ten-year-old Roy Chandler pointed out the famous mobster Al Capone to his eight-year-old sister, Barbara. Their mother couldn't resist snapping a photo, even though Warden Johnston had strictly forbidden the use of cameras.

Their father's first assignment was guard duty in the tower overlooking the west side of the island. Barbara liked to deliver lunch to him. Afterward she would dawdle

Above: *This photo of the new prisoners arriving by train was taken from the balcony of Building 64 by Mrs. Chandler with her Brownie camera.*

along the fence, even though she'd been instructed not to. One day her father sent down a warning note in a bucket on a rope that was used to carry messages down from the tower. "Don't go near the fence! Al Capone is there." Barbara threw down the note and ran home. But her brother was thrilled when his father later introduced him to the mobster after Roy got his asthma shot in the prison's clinic. Shivers ran down his spine when Capone shook his hand. Roy later renamed himself Rocky after his childhood home and wrote a book with his father about Alcatraz.

At the end of that summer Wanda Harrington returned from her vacation and started up the road to the lighthouse to find her friend Jacquie Schneider. Guards stopped her, insisting she first go through the electric eye in the registration office. Wanda and Jacquie were confused by all the new rules and dearly missed their army friends.

Above: Roy and Barbara Chandler on the porch of Building 64 in February 1935.

Right: All residents needed to check in at the registration office and show their identification card when leaving and returning to the island.

STUCKER CHARLES E

PERMANENT RESIDENT

Name STUCKER, CHARLES E.

Title	Relation Son of Lieut.
Res. No.	Date of Birth May 7, 1940
Comp. Fair	Hair Blonde
Eyes Blue	Height 5' 3"
Weight 100	Phone

FPI INC ERO-10-11-44-750-1810-51

FAMILY LIFE ON THE ROCK

During the federal prison era, sixty guard families and ten bachelor guards lived on the island. Each year upward of seventy children tore across the old military parade ground playing tag, baseball, football, and a game called *prisoner*. "It was always better to be a guard than a convict!" declared Ernie Lageson Jr., the son of a prison guard. Families lived a quarter mile below the cell house, but didn't worry about the convicts and never locked their doors. The mothers said, "At least we know where the bad guys are." Parents were more concerned about the safety of their children playing on the steep cliffs.

Tots to teenagers played on the abandoned military cannons around the island and hung out in the canteen, post office, and bowling alley where twelve-year-old Anna Tolksdorf got paid a nickel to set pins all evening.

Top: *Like Barbara and Roy Chandler and Charlie Ping, Alcatraz kids often played on the dangerous cliffs, which worried their mothers more than their proximity to criminals.*

Middle: *The island had its own bowling alley.*

Left: *Bob Orr, Don Martin, Don Fowler, and Op Flint straddle one of the abandoned cannons around the island.*

This aerial view shows the new family apartment buildings (in the left foreground) built in the early 1940s.

In the early years the families had no telephones, so girls like Bev Stucker had to put up with the guards' teasing when she hiked up to the prison to take a call from her boyfriend in San Francisco.

Families celebrated the end of summer with a watermelon feed on the dock. On Christmas Eve the children caroled around the island, including outside the unusually quiet prison. Afterward they stopped by the warden's house for cookies, hot chocolate, and a visit from Santa. On holidays families were allowed inside the prison theater to view the same G-rated movie the prisoners had seen that afternoon. By the 1940s the movies were shown in the social hall.

Every Halloween children dressed up and trick-or-treated at the family residences. Years later, Alcatraz kids brought their own children back to continue the tradition.

RULES, RULES, RULES

The prison housed far more dangerous criminals than during the military years, so security was much tighter. The kids sometimes complained that they had more rules than the inmates. Children were to stay away from the cliffs, beaches, and fenced areas around the prison. Kids often forgot that with guard towers all around the island, prisoners weren't the only ones being watched. Once during low tide, thirteen-year-old Don Martin Jr. and his friends snuck over to a cave on the west side of the island. The boys rushed home when they finally noticed the watch tower looming above them.

The prisoners weren't the only island residents being watched by the guard towers circa 1953.

Kids observed prisoners working down on the dock in front of the registration office or near the family quarters.

"We didn't want the guard shooting at us, thinking we were escaped convicts!" Don explained.

Soon after the prison opened, Warden Johnston decided all toy guns needed to be confiscated. Guards gathered them up and loaded the toy guns into the back of a truck carrying some prisoners. As the truck drove away, the prisoners threw the guns back to the kids! Then the kids hid them away from their parents and the warden.

Families were not to talk to anyone, even relatives, about life on Alcatraz. Pat Bergen got punished for lying to classmates about a pretend tunnel that ran under the

The children were fair game for reporters when they came off the boat in San Francisco.

bay to Alcatraz. Reporters tried to talk to the young people as they came off the boat in San Francisco to attend school. Most of the kids ignored the questions, but Roy Chandler and his buddies described the dungeon where criminals survived on bread and water alone. Others told tall tales, too, and snickered when their stories appeared in the newspaper. But laughter turned to tears when their fathers were called into the warden's office.

PRISONERS AND THE KIDS

The children were taught to stay away from the few prisoners allowed to work around the island. Sometimes these inmates picked up news about the families. One told Joyce Rose's father about her boyfriends. Another inmate wished Don Martin Jr. a happy birthday and gave him a flower. If the kids threw a candy bar to a prisoner, a ball recovered by the prison workers from the beach or up by the cellhouse would be thrown back. An inmate on garbage detail gave nine-year-old Billy Hart his first baseball mitt. "We never got to talk, but I got to know that convict just the same," he said.

The prisoners were concerned about Joyce Rose's love life (far right) and all her friends in the "Just Us Girls" Club (JUG).

The gumball machine outside the corner store in Building 64 was a favorite of all the kids.

Billy later got punished for giving prisoners bubblegum, which they then used in slingshots fired at the guards.

Inmates could not receive letters from their own children. The only young people ever allowed to visit were Mark Sobell and his stepsister, Sydney. Their father, Morton Sobell, had been convicted of conspiracy to commit espionage for Russia during the cold war, along with Julius and Ethel Rosenberg. When the Bureau of Prisons ruled it was harmful for children to visit parents in prison, their mother, Helen, found a well-known psychiatrist who said not being able to visit was more damaging.

Twelve-year-old Sydney was frightened by the security check-in at the prison and today advocates for children with parents in prison. Five-year-old Mark remembers looking through a pane of glass and talking to his dad on a telephone. "It was a pretty sad way to get to know your father. When he got out of prison, we were strangers."

As shown in this newspaper article, the Alcatraz guard refused to let Mrs. Helen Sobell and son, Mark, board the boat for Alcatraz in 1955. Mrs. Sobell finally won permission for the children to visit their father.

NO TRIP—The faces of Mrs. Helen Sobell and her son, Mark, mirror their disappointment yesterday as they learn that their planned visit to the husband and father, Morton Sobell, sentenced to Alcatraz as a spy, has been denied. The Alcatraz guard at the boat landing at the foot of Van Ness Avenue refused to give his name. Mrs. Sobell will be allowed to visit her husband, but the boy cannot go on the "Rock."

The Army Returns 1941-45

After the United States declared war against Japan and Germany in December 1941, Alcatraz was fortified again for the first time since 1907. Soldiers returned to the island and antiaircraft guns were mounted on the cell house and apartment building roofs. Nine-year-old Pat and her father, Phil Bergen, made sure all the families pulled

down their dark green blackout curtains every evening. Even the lighthouse and the prison lights were turned off, so the Japanese could not drop a bomb on Alcatraz. Families gathered regularly for air raid drills in the basement of Building 64, nicknamed "Chinatown." They sat on the seawall and looked for signs of Japanese submarines out in the bay and watched ace pilot Jimmy Doolittle practice loops overhead for his bombing missions over Tokyo.

The younger girls like Kay Bergen and her friends brought their hamsters and guinea pigs up to the solarium to help the soldiers pass the time. The teenage girls flirted with the soldiers and invited them to their dances. The teenage boys rushed to enlist but had trouble explaining their childhood home. When asked where he grew up, Private First Class Herb Faulk responded, "Alcatraz Island, Sir." His commanding officer barked back, "Don't get smart with me, soldier!"

Nine-year-old Bill Dolby arrived on Alcatraz in 1944. With the soldiers, antiaircraft guns, and convoys of ships headed in and out of the bay, he felt like he was smack-dab in the middle of the war. When the war ended, Bill and all the kids held up WELCOME HOME signs for returning ships passing through the Golden Gate.

Left: *"Chinatown," where the families gathered for air raid drills and the kids played hide-and-seek.*

Right: *Bill Dolby (fourth from left) and his friends played football on the parade ground with a white ball so they could see it in foggy weather.*

SIEGE OF 1946

Nothing rocked the island like the three-day siege of May 1946. After school on Thursday, May 2, seventh-grader Ernie Lageson Jr. studied the front page of San Francisco's News *Call Bulletin* before starting his paper route. Under breaking news, a small box noted that at 1:30 p.m. six Alcatraz inmates had broken into the gun gallery. But it wasn't until later that evening Ernie discovered they had taken over the cell house where his dad was on duty.

No one was allowed to return to the island, so the Red Cross booked hotel rooms for the stranded mothers and excited schoolchildren. But as hours turned into days, the kids grew worried about their fathers' safety. That first evening Ernie Lageson and his mother perched by the radio, anxious for news. Six-year-old Chuck Stucker stood with his mother on the Fort Mason dock as she begged officials for news of her husband. Chuck and his family didn't learn until after the siege that his father had been locked in a cell with eighteen inmates for forty-eight hours.

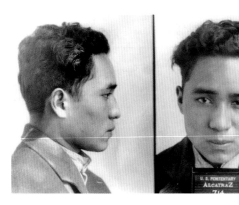

Top, right: *Twelve-year-old Ernie Lageson Jr. with his parents in a 1946 family photo.*

Middle: *Clarence Carnes, the youngest prison-era inmate, was persuaded to help the ringleaders of the siege. All the others were executed, but due to his age, Carnes was given life imprisonment and sent to solitary confinement, where he roomed next to Robert Stroud, the Birdman of Alcatraz.*

Bottom: *Chuck Stucker's father was held captive for two days during the siege. Chuck is shown here with his uncle, Nova Stucker, associate warden, circa 1950.*

In the end fifteen guards and one inmate were wounded, and two guards and three inmates lost their lives. Fifteen-year-old Bob Stites didn't find out that his father had been killed until the second afternoon. The Stites were devastated, especially Bob's ten-year-old brother, Herb.

Warden James A. Johnston leads a memorial service for Officer Harold P. Stites on October 1, 1946. U.S. Attorney General Tom Clark has his arm around Herbert Stites, 10. On his other side are Mrs. Stites, and Robert, 15.

Holding newspaper is marine C. L. Buckner, who helped in the action.

Thirteen-year-old Joan Marie Miller and her ten-year-old brother, Billy, learned of their father's death during the Friday afternoon rosary at St. Brigid's Church. After the funerals, both families had to move off Alcatraz. The island community took up a collection for the widows and their children. Ernie Lageson Jr. later wrote a book about the whole ordeal.

LIFE AND LOVE ON THE ROCK

Over the years families came and went, but the community remained close. Some people remained only a short time and others for decades. Two families cover the entire span of the federal years. The Faulks were one of the first to arrive in 1934 and stayed until 1953. As youngsters Ruth Faulk and Gayle Wiley, the lighthouse keeper's son, played together. As teenagers they fell in love and later married. The Harts arrived in 1948 and raised five kids on the Rock. Islanders celebrated Betty Hart's wedding to guard Dick Barnett in 1955. The young couple stayed and started a family with youngsters, David and Cindy.

Above: *Herbert, Ruth, and Eddy (in sailor suit) Faulk, and their parents spent almost two decades on the Rock.*

Right: *Christmas 1949 with the Hart family in their apartment in Building 64. Front row: Bud and Barbara; second row: Bobby and Betty with parents; third row: Billy.*

'I'M FROM ALCATRAZ'—John Brunner, 12, who lives on Alcatraz where his father is an electrical engineer, displays a picture of the island at the Boy Scout Jamboree. He brought genuine rocks from "The Rock" for swapping purposes and a picture of himself on Alcatraz to convince skeptical fellow Scouts that he does live on the island in San Francisco Bay.

In every era Alcatraz kids were peppered with questions about their mysterious home. *Collier's* magazine published a photo spread on the children in 1953, surprising its readers with the news that kids actually lived there. John Brunner showed off a piece of the Rock at the 1953 Boy Scout Jamboree. Bob Orr invited his Sacred Heart High School teachers out to visit. Teenagers sometimes felt confined on the small island. In foggy weather they spooked one another on the roads and parade ground. In rough weather they rode the boat back and forth to San Francisco to see who got seasick first.

Caught up in their own lives, the guards' children never thought about the pressure their fathers were under, and the fathers never discussed their work at home. They didn't even mention murderer Robert Stroud, who was reported to have been the meanest inmate ever. Made famous by the movie *The Birdman of Alcatraz,* Stroud had kept birds earlier at the Leavenworth Penitentiary but was never actually allowed to keep them on Alcatraz.

Senior finds commuting to SH from Alcatraz a problem

By FRANK MARINO

Have you ever been to Alcatraz Island? Not many of us have, but we have a member of the student body, Bob Orr of class S-202c, who LIVES (We'd better get it straight the very first that Bob [the "Rock" by choice and necessity!)

Anyway, we got to won what life was like on Al who lived there, what th and so on, and so we g to give us a little informa the place.

Alcatraz isn't very la islands go, being only 16 long and rising a maxin 130 feet above the waters Francisco Bay. It was f by the Spaniards original in 1858 it began to be t house military prisoners US government. In 1933 came a maximum custod eral prison and has remai In spite of recent rumors would be closed as a pris converted into a sort of Sa cisco "Disneyland."

Life On The Rock

What's it like on the "l Bob's father is a prison g one of the sixty or so

walls. There is also a post office and a grocery store on the island. Bob works in the latter after school.

"Rock" (the others go to Galile High) are seldom late to class That's one bus you either mak or you don't!

Above: *John Brunner, featured in local newspapers, shows off the island at the Boy Scout Jamboree.*

Right: *A school newspaper article featured Bob Orr's challenging commute to Sacred Heart High School in San Francisco.*

Photo of cable car on Powell-Hyde line with City Visitors' Bureau envoys Kathleen and Maureen Hazelton. The island in the middle of the bay could be seen from all over the city, sparking curiosity.

Escape from Alcatraz 1962

Some prisoners were still kids themselves when they started committing crimes. Frank Morris first went behind bars at age thirteen and attempted many escapes, including Alcatraz's most famous: On the evening of June 11, 1962, fifteen-year-old Jolene Dollison went to bed at about the same time Frank Morris and Clarence and John Anglin began the breakout they had planned for a year. The next morning Jolene awoke to the blare of the escape siren and guards searching every inch of the island. Her father, the acting warden, requested help from police dogs in San Francisco. When they arrived excited children began playing with the dogs helping the kids to forget all about the missing prisoners.

News of the clever escape went around the world; it marked the fourteenth escape attempt at Alcatraz since 1936. Jolene Dollison later wrote a book about this escape, concluding that the prisoners could not have survived the tides and freezing water. The National Park Service agrees.

Above: *A teenager at the time of the escape, Jolene Dollison later wrote a book about the breakout.*

Left: *Frank Morris is pictured here in reform school at age fourteen.*

43

But no bodies were ever found and no one really knows what happened to these men. The movie *Escape from Alcatraz* dramatizes a successful getaway.

Later some guards admitted that recently relaxed security procedures had enabled the three convicts to pull off their plan. Shortly before their escape attempt, Attorney General Robert Kennedy had announced that the prison would close the following year.

Left: *Movie poster from 1979 movie* Escape from Alcatraz.

Right: *Morris and the Anglins were never seen again after the escape. It's unknown whether they survived.*

WANTED BY THE FBI

ESCAPED FEDERAL PRISONER — BANK ROBBER
JOHN WILLIAM ANGLIN

FBI No. 4,745,119

Photographs taken 1960

DESCRIPTION

Age:	32, born May 2, 1930, Donalsonville, Georgia (not supported by birth records)
Height:	5'10"	**Complexion:** Ruddy
Weight:	140 pounds	**Race:** White
Build:	Medium	**Nationality:** American
Eyes:	Blue	**Occupations:** Farmer, laborer
Hair:	Blond	

Scars and Marks: Scar left side of forehead, left forearm near wrist, scar left side of abdomen, small scar left cheek

Fingerprint Classification:

CRIMINAL RECORD

Anglin has been convicted of gra...

CAUTION

ANGLIN HAS BEEN CONVICTED OF BANK...
OF FIREARMS WHEN LAST ARRESTED. H...
TEMPTED ESCAPE. CONSIDER EXTREME...

A Federal warrant was issued on June 13, 1962, a...
escaping from the Federal Penitentiary at Alcatraz...

**IF YOU HAVE INFORMATION CONCERNING THI...
YOUR LOCAL FBI OFFICE. TELEPHONE NUMBE...**

Wanted Flyer No. 306
June 14, 1962

CALL SAN
FRA-CISCO
KL 2-2155

WANTED BY THE FBI

ESCAPED FEDERAL PRISONER — BANK ROBBER
CLARENCE ANGLIN

FBI No. 4,731,702

Photograph taken 1960   Photographs taken 1958

DESCRIPTION

Age:	31, born May 11, 1931, Donalsonville, Georgia (not supported by birth records)
Height:	5'11"	**Complexion:** Light
Weight:	160 to 168 pounds	**Race:** White
Build:	Medium	**Nationality:** American
Hair:	Brown	**Occupations:** Cabinet maker, farmer, laborer
Eyes:	Hazel	

Scars and Marks: ...upper lip, scar between eyes, scar right forearm, ...ZONA" and scroll left arm, "NITA" upper right arm

18 O 27 W 100 21
L 27 W 010

CRIMINAL RECORD

...burglary, bank robbery and attempted escape.

CAUTION

...BANK ROBBERY AND WAS IN POSSESSION OF...
...HE HAS A PREVIOUS RECORD OF ESCAPES.
...S.

...62, at San Francisco, California, charging Anglin with
...atraz in violation of Title 18, U. S. Code, Section 751.

...THIS PERSON, PLEASE NOTIFY ME OR CONTACT
...MBER IS LISTED BELOW.

DIRECTOR
FEDERAL BUREAU OF INVESTIGATION
UNITED STATES DEPARTMENT OF JUSTICE
WASHINGTON 25, D. C.
TELEPHONE, NATIONAL 8-7117

WANTED BY THE FBI

ESCAPED FEDERAL PRISONER
FRANK LEE MORRIS

Photographs taken 1960   FBI No. 2,157,606

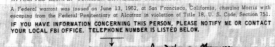

Aliases: Carl Cecil Clark, Frank Laine, Frank Lane, Frank William Lyons, Frankie Lyons, Stanley O'Neal Singletary, and others

DESCRIPTION

Age:	35, born September 1, 1926, Washington, D. C.
Height:	5'7½"	**Complexion:** Ruddy
Weight:	135 pounds	**Race:** White
Build:	Medium	**Nationality:** American
Hair:	Brown	**Occupations:** Car salesman, draftsman, painter
Eyes:	Hazel	

Scars and Marks: Numerous tattoo including devil's head upper right arm, star base of left thumb, "13" base of left index finger

Fingerprint Classification: 22 M 9 U I00 12
L I U 000

CRIMINAL RECORD

Morris has been convicted of burglary, larceny of an automobile, grand larceny, possession of narcotics, bank burglary, armed robbery and escape.

CAUTION

MORRIS HAS BEEN REPORTED TO BE ARMED IN THE PAST AND HAS A PREVIOUS RECORD OF ATTEMPTED ESCAPE. CONSIDER EXTREMELY DANGEROUS.

A Federal warrant was issued on June 13, 1962, at San Francisco, California, charging Morris with escaping from the Federal Penitentiary at Alcatraz in violation of Title 18, U. S. Code, Section 751.

IF YOU HAVE INFORMATION CONCERNING THIS PERSON, PLEASE NOTIFY ME OR CONTACT YOUR LOCAL FBI OFFICE. TELEPHONE NUMBER IS LISTED BELOW.

DIRECTOR
FEDERAL BUREAU OF INVESTIGATION
UNITED STATES DEPARTMENT OF JUSTICE
WASHINGTON 25, D. C.
TELEPHONE, NATIONAL 8-7117

Wanted Flyer No. 307
June 14, 1962

CALL SAN
FRANCISCO
KL 2-2155

ISLAND IN TRANSITION

1963-69

DUE TO STRUCTURAL decay Alcatraz had become too expensive to operate and keep secure. So in March 1963 inmates were transferred to other maximum-security prisons and the families of the guards departed. When the lighthouse became automated in November 1963, the lighthouse keepers' families left, too. The parade ground stood eerily quiet after more than a century of kids living on the Rock.

Former guard Jack Hart and his wife, Marie, stayed on as caretakers, their five children already grown. Sons Bud and Bill soon returned to help out. "I saw far more of the island as a caretaker than I ever did as a kid. But the prison still spooked me," Bud reported.

Left: *An artist's rendering of a proposed space travel theme park design, one of many options considered for the abandoned island.*

Lori Brosnan (far left) visited the island as a third grader. Today, she's the longest serving park ranger on Alcatraz.

San Franciscans debated the future of the island. Proposals included a UN peace memorial, a second Statue of Liberty, a bird sanctuary, a wax museum, and even a gambling casino. When billionaire Lamar Hunt proposed to build a space travel theme park, outraged citizens protested. So the Harts remained and their youngest child, Barbara, got married on the island in 1966 at the only home she'd ever known.

Third-grader Lori Brosnan visited in 1968 with her father, who was making a documentary for the government. Lori, her brother, and friend Sarah played with the guard dogs, Duffy and Duke, ate lunch in the warden's house, and ran around the prisoners' recreation yard. Lori never forgot her afternoon on the Rock and twenty years later called her father to announce she'd just been hired to be a park ranger on Alcatraz.

INDIAN OCCUPATION
November 1969-June 1971

IN THE DARK OF NIGHT on November 20, 1969, sixty-eight unarmed Native American adults and children peacefully landed on Alcatraz to protest two centuries of broken Indian treaties, neglect, and mistreatment by the U.S. government. Protestors laid claim to Alcatraz under the right of discovery; Indians had been on this land long before white people. While the adults held meetings, the kids explored the island, running across the rooftops and playing Indians vs. the Feds on the parade

Boys playing on an old abandoned tractor.

A.William ("Tinky") Lopez and Michael Moppin run along the island's shore, with the Bay Bridge in the distance.

ground. Teenagers holed up in the dank prison cells and told ghost stories by candle-light. Two-year-old Deynon Means didn't want to sleep in the spooky prison, so he and his mother, LaNada Boyer, stayed in the warden's house.

For months, fourteen-year-old Adam Robert Nordwall Jr. had watched his Ojibwa father, Adam Fortunate Eagle Nordwall, a Bay Area Indian leader, write and rewrite

a document entitled "Proclamation from the Indians of All Tribes." The morning after the landing, Mohawk leader Richard Oakes read the proclamation for the press. "We, the Native Americans, reclaim the land known as Alcatraz Island . . . by right of discovery. . . . This tiny island will be a symbol of the great lands once ruled by free and noble Indians."

Supporters began donating money and food. Everyone, young and old, helped out. Julie Nordwall loved working in the communal kitchen, so different from life at Marina [California] High School, where she and her brother, Adam, had been the only Indians. In the guard towers teenagers kept lookout for Coast Guard boats circling the island. Occupation leaders feared the government might try to remove them. Five days into the Occupation, local restaurant owners provided a huge Thanksgiving feast for over four hundred people.

Above: *All the kids looked up to leader Richard Oakes, pictured here on the dock with Deynon Means, whom the press dubbed the Alcatraz Kid.*

Right: *Standing in line for the Thanksgiving feast, dancers Leonard Harrison, Julie Nordwall, and Adam Fortunate Eagle Nordwall.*

The Return of Diamond Island

Former Alcatraz prisoner Clarence Carnes's Choctaw mother and sisters attended the feast to honor Alcatraz as a place of healing instead of despair. A powwow followed with dancers like teenage Nez Perce brothers Mike and Zack Ellenwood joining in. Elders, like Mike and Zack's grandmother, found hope that Indians could still dance and sing after all that had been taken from the tribes.

Eleven-year-old Ed Willie's family came to get away from their gang-infested neighborhood in Oakland, California. Even though

Ed had at one time lived on his father's Paiute reservation in Nevada, he didn't feel like an Indian. But on Alcatraz, surrounded by Indians of many tribes, he finally felt like he belonged. Ed, his brother, Elvin, and their buddies watched John Trudell record his daily *Radio Free Alcatraz* broadcast in the old movie theater. Everyone celebrated the birth of John and Lu Trudell's son, Wovoka, in July, the only known Indian baby ever born on Alcatraz.

Above, right: Former prisoner Clarence Carnes, who took part in the 1946 siege (see page 38), visits his old cell, #25, in August 1980

Left: This boy played chess in a cell. Other teens enjoyed trying to figure out where infamous prisoners like Al Capone and the Birdman of Alcatraz might have slept.

Ed's fifteen-year-old sister, Karen, met her future husband, Larry Harrison, on the island. Ed's five-year-old sister, Lisa, made stick houses on the beach with new friends Benjamin, Peter, Georgia, and Nadya Bratt and the Lopez kids. Eldie Bratt, a Quechua-Aymara La Banda Indian from Peru, helped keep track of all the young people on the island, along with her own four children. Actor Benjamin Bratt and filmmaker Peter Bratt believe protesting with their mother as youngsters influences the types of movies they make today.

Top: *Eldie Bratt, a Peruvian Indian, brought her children over from San Francisco and watched over the young people whose parents needed to be at work or college classes.*

Left: *Benjamin Bratt at the San Francisco Indian Center.*

Above, Right: *Peter Bratt with his sister Georgia on his left, little sister Veruschka behind him, and friend Kim Contreras on his right.*

INDIANS OF ALL TRIBES

During the eighteen-month protest, 16,000 Indians from almost one hundred tribes arrived from cities and Indian reservations across the country. Some visited for the day; others stayed weeks or even months. Cree singer Buffy St. Marie gave a concert and young dancers like Adam Nordwall Jr. joined in the celebration. On the first anniversary of the Occupation LaNada Boyer and other leaders announced their plan to start a university for Indian students.

As children many of the protestors had attended government boarding schools where they learned nothing about their own people. So on the island students studied their tribal culture and crafts along with reading, writing, and math. At night around the campfire the kids participated in drumming, dancing, and storytelling.

The Occupation leaders faced many challenges. A fire in May 1970 destroyed the warden's house, officers' club, lighthouse

Top: *Indian tipi with Golden Gate Bridge in background stood as a powerful symbol of Indian culture during the Occupation.*

Above, left: *People liked to gather around communal bonfires outside the prison in the evenings.*

quarters, and temporarily shut down the lighthouse. The cause was undetermined, but some people blamed the Indians for the fire and public support for their cause waned. Government officials cut off the water barge to try and force the protestors to vacate the island. But the Indians stayed, transporting water in jugs by private boats. The biggest blow came with the death of Richard Oakes's stepdaughter Yvonne from a fall in an apartment stairway. Yvonne's friends on the island attended her funeral in San Francisco. Richard and his family departed, never to return. Some of the original protestors and their children began leaving, too, due to the tough living conditions or the need to return to college classes and jobs. A few like Deynon Means and his mother remained the entire time.

THE PROTEST LIVES ON

At dawn on June 11, 1971, Sioux teenager Peggy Lee stood in front of the cell house, watching the sun come up. When she heard a motorboat down by the dock, she watched as federal marshals with guns stormed up the hill. The younger kids ran around the cell house, and later, down on the dock, tried to push the agents into the water. Eventually all the protesters were forced to board the boats and were brought to San Francisco. But their political activism didn't end. Many joined new occupations and marches around the country. A few months later, on a protest trip to South Dakota, Peggy Lee met her future husband, Mike Ellenwood, another Alcatraz teenager.

In the end the Indians of All Tribes didn't get to keep the island, but much was gained. Because of Alcatraz and later protests, Americans became more aware of the wrongs done to Indians. President Nixon finally ended the 1958 Termination and Relocation policies, which forced Indian tribes off the reservations and into large cities, far away from their tribal lands. Congress increased funding for Indian health care and education. Most important, young Indians learned firsthand that change was possible.

K. Longria participated in the Occupation with her mother. "As a young girl I didn't understand why we had to keep attending all these protests. Today I realize how important it was, not only to my people but to the world in general."

Harold Patty (Pauite), Oohosie (Cree), Peggy Lee (Sioux), and Sandy Berger (Nez Perce) promised to keep fighting for Indian rights on the last day of the Occupation, June 11, 1971.

NATIONAL HISTORICAL PARK
1972–Present

S OON AFTER THE INDIANS were removed, federal officials began bulldozing island buildings to prevent another takeover.
Again local citizens protested and the demolition ended, but not
before the apartments were turned into rubble. In 1972 Congress
created the Golden Gate National Recreation Area, which includes
Alcatraz. Twelve-year-old Michael Esslinger visited soon after the
park opened to the public in 1973 and met Clarence Carnes, who
shared with visitors his experiences as the youngest Alcatraz prison
era inmate. Michael became determined to learn everything he could
about the prison's history and twenty-five years later published a book
on the subject. In 1976 thirteen-year-old John Cantwell worked in the

Right: *Ranger John Cantwell worked in the island bookstore as a teen.*
Today he enjoys sharing his knowledge of island history with visitors.

island bookstore for $2.50 an hour and dreamed of giving tours on the island. The next year he got hired as a part-time seasonal ranger and has worked for the park service ever since.

In spite of the hordes of visitors, the island is once again home to thousands of nesting birds. Sea life thrives in the tidal pools, and monarch butterflies still stop every fall on their migration west.

Since 1972, every Thanksgiving at dawn, thousands celebrate the "Unthanksgiving" ceremony, commemorating the Indian Occupation with speeches and songs. Belva Cottier Belgas returns to show her children the place where she played as a girl while her mother and grandmother participated in the protest.

And every year hundreds of swimmers train to attempt the challenging and chilly one-and-one-quarter-mile swim from Alcatraz to San Francisco. In October 2005 fourth-grader Johnny Wilson became one of the youngest swimmers ever to accomplish the feat, while raising $30,000 for the victims of Hurricane Katrina.

Top, right: *Twelve-year-old visitor Mariah Easton of New Jersey was struck by the cramped cells the prisoners lived in and the view of San Francisco that must have tempted them to escape.*

Middle, left: *Oglala Sioux Belva Cottier Belgas (front right) with her mother, husband, and children at the Unthanksgiving ceremony 2004.*

Bottom, right: *Young swimmer Johnny Wilson (center) and his friends helped raise money for victims of Hurricane Katrina.*

ALCATRAZ KIDS GROW UP

THE ALCATRAZ Alumni Association holds a reunion on the Rock every August. Almost all the inmates, guards, and wives are gone now, but their children carry on the tradition. For many these early experiences influenced their adult lives. Several have written books about Alcatraz. Modern-day ambassador Chuck Stucker returns often to the Rock, sharing his photos and stories from all eras of the island's history with eager visitors.

Some Alcatraz kids married their childhood sweethearts, so their memories are doubly rich. Others, like

Edy Lynch, a former Military-era kid, shows off her childhood home with her step-great-grandson Hunter during an alumni reunion.

Bobby Stewart, John Brunner, Bill Dolby, and Bob Stites pursued careers in the military. Many, like Bob and Barbara Hart and Bob Orr went into law enforcement or prison work. Teacher Brian Hack entertains his Roseville [California] High School students with stories of growing up on Alcatraz in the early sixties and the island's place in history.

As adults many of the kids who participated in the Indian Occupation have worked for better Indian services, such as Lisa Willie and her sister Karen in health care. When Wilma Mankiller brought her young daughters, Gina and Felicia, out to the 1969 Occupation, it ignited a passion for her Cherokee people that led her to become their first woman chief in 1985. Like so many Alcatraz kids, Jon Bellanger's memories of the island remain strong. A member of the Kickapoo tribe, he took part in the protest as a child and today works with Indian youth in Oakland, California. "I tell them not to forget who they are. You can't know your future if you don't know your past."

Above: Former Alcatraz kids (from left to right): Bud Hart, Bob Orr, Ed Faulk, and Chuck Stucker, shown with the author during a research trip to the island.

FURTHER RESOURCES

Books

Babyak, Jolene. *Breaking the Rock: The Great Escapes from Alcatraz*. Berkeley, CA: Ariel Vamp Press, 2001.

_____. *Birdman: The Many Faces of Robert Stroud*. Berkeley, CA: Ariel Vamp Press, 1994.

_____. *Eyewitness on Alcatraz: Interviews with Guards, Families, and Prisoners Who Live on the Rock*. Berkeley, CA: Ariel Vamp Press, 1988.

Bunting, Eve. *Someone Is Hiding on Alcatraz Island*. New York: Berkley Publishing Group, reissue edition, 1994.

Chandler, Roy F., and E. F. Chandler. *Alcatraz: The Hardest Years 1934-1938*. Jacksonville, NC: Iron Brigade Amory Publishers, 1989.

Choldenko, Gennifer. *Al Capone Does My Shirts*. New York: G.P. Putnam, 2004.

Fortunate Eagle, Adam. *Heart of the Rock*. Norman, OK: University of Oklahoma Press, 2002.

Johnson, Troy. *The Occupation of Alcatraz Island*. Chicago, IL: University of Illinois Press, 1996.

Esslinger, Michael. *Alcatraz: A Definitive History of the Penitentiary Years*. San Francisco, CA: Ocean View Publishing, 2003.

George, Linda. *Alcatraz: Cornerstone of Freedom*. Children's Press, 1999.

Lageson Jr., Ernest B. *Battle at Alcatraz: A Desperate Attempt to Escape the Rock*. Omaha Nebraska: Addicus Books, Inc., 1999.

Martini, John A. *Fortress Alcatraz: Guardian of the Golden Gate*. Kailua, Hawaii: Pacific Monograph, 1990.

Odier, Pierre. *The Rock: A History of Alcatraz — The Fort, The Prison*. Eagle Rock, CA: L'Image Odier, 1997.

Quillen, Jim. *Alcatraz from the Inside*. Golden Gate Parks Association, 1991.

Weintraub, Aileen. *Alcatraz Island Light: The West Coast's First Lighthouse*. New York: PowerKids Press, 2003.

VIDEOS

Alcatraz Is Not an Island, Turtle Island Productions, 2001, narrated by Benjamin Bratt.

Children of Alcatraz, Independent Productions, Zia Films, 2004.

Lonely Island: Hidden Alcatraz, KQED, 2003.

Secrets of Alcatraz, KQED, GGNRA, 1996.

WEB SITES

www.nps.gov/alcatraz/tours

www.alcatrazhistory.com

www.pbs.org/itvs/alcatrazisnotanisland/alcatraz.html (background information and interactive lesson plans)

www.kqed.org/w/alcatraz/resources.html (terrific history references)

www.militarymuseum.org/Alcatraz.html (military history of island)

www.alcatrazalumni.org (information on people who lived on the island)

www.baymodel.org (information on the ecological environment, history, and culture of the San Francisco Bay)

www.alcatrazchallenge.com (information on swimming from the island)

ALCATRAZ TIMELINE

1775 Spanish sailors discover and name the island *La Isla de los Alcatraces.*

1848 United States gains control of California.

1854 Construction begins on army post on Alcatraz.

1854 *June 1* – lighthouse begins operation and lighthouse keepers and families arrive.

1859 Post on Alcatraces is completed; soldiers and families move onto the island.

1894-95 Hopi Indians are imprisoned on the island.

1899 Number of military prisoners jumps from 25 to 440.

1905 New cell house and lighthouse construction begins.

1907 Military fort is closed down. Island is renamed the Disciplinary Barracks on Alcatraz and becomes a minimum-security prison.

1909 New lighthouse and new cell house for four hundred prisoners begin operations.

1934 Disciplinary Barracks closes in April.

1963 Lighthouse and foghorns become automated, and federal prison is closed.

1963-69 Island is unoccupied.

1969 *November 20* – Indians successfully occupy the island.

1970 President Nixon rescinds the Indian Policy of Relocation and Termination.

1971 *June 11* – Federal agents remove remaining Indians.

1972 *May 31* – Federal government declares Alcatraz a historic park, part of the Golden Gate National Recreation Area.

1973 Tourists begin visiting the Rock.

INDEX